PRINTING

Hilary Devonshire

Photography: Chris Fairclough

FRANKLIN WATTS
London/New York/Sydney/Toronto

Franklin Watts
96 Leonard Street
London EC2A 4RH

Franklin Watts Australia
14 Mars Road
Lane Cove
NSW 2066

ISBN: Paperback edition 0 7496 0483 2
        Hardback edition 0 86313 708 3

Paperback edition 1991

Hardback edition published
in the Fresh Start series.

Editor: Jenny Wood

Design: Edward Kinsey

Printed in Belgium

The author wishes to
record her thanks in the
preparation of this book
to: Henry Pluckrose for
his advice and guidance;
Christopher Fairclough
for the excellence of his
step-by-step
photographs; and
Chester Fisher, Franklin
Watts Ltd.

Contents

Equipment and materials

This book describes activities which use the following:

Brushes for glue and paint
Card (thick and thin, manilla)
Cardboard tubes
Corrugated card
Drawing inks
Felt
Glue (acrylic PVA, or similar)
Junk materials (e.g. matches, corks, pipe-cleaners, scraps of fabric, small pieces of wood)
Modelling clay
Modelling tool (or lollipop stick or teaspoon)
Old rags
Paint (poster or powder paint, ready mixed)
Paper – cartridge paper or good quality typing paper
  – sugar or construction paper
  – tissue paper
Paper clips

Paper towels
Pencil
Pens (ballpoint and felt-tip)
Plastic trays
Polystyrene tile
Printing inks (water-based inks are preferable as they can be washed out easily)
Printing pads (make your own from a saucer containing a piece of sponge or thick cloth soaked with paint)
Printing rollers (obtainable from artists' materials stockists)
Printing sheets (e.g. plastic, glass, or formica – these provide a flat, smooth surface for spreading the ink evenly)
Saucers (old)
Scissors
Sponges
String

Getting ready

Printing is a way of transferring identical images from one surface to another. Familiar examples are printed patterns on materials and wallpapers in which the designs are often repeated many times.

This book suggests a number of ways in which you can try out different printing ideas. You do not need a lot of sophisticated materials – anything with an interesting surface texture will print. When you begin to experiment (and I hope this book will encourage you to do so) you will discover that collecting materials, preparing them for printing, and making prints are as fascinating as actually seeing the finished result.

One of the most pleasing things about printing is that you do not have to be able to draw well to create pictures. You will be able to produce many patterns and images from the ideas in the following pages, and the most exciting aspect about the prints you will make is that they will all be different and often totally unexpected!

Some hints

Printing need not be a messy activity so long as you are well prepared. Have some old newspaper ready so that you can cover the table and floor, a large, old shirt or blouse to protect your clothes, and some old, damp rags to keep your hands clean.

Before you start to print, you must decide which type of paper to use. There are many different types of paper, each with a different texture and thickness. Each type will give a different effect, so you will need to experiment. Don't forget too that you can use different colours of papers and that it is fun to experiment with the unusual – for example, white paper towels (very absorbent), damp paper or thin, tissue paper.

As you work, you will discover how the materials behave – how thin or thick you need the paints or ink, which tools are best, which papers to choose. You can learn these things only by trying them out for yourself. Have fun!

Hand prints

To make a hand print you will need a printing sheet (see page 4), a roller, paint or printing ink, a plastic tray, and paper.

When you have made some prints, experiment by making prints in several colours. You could even try taking a print of your foot!

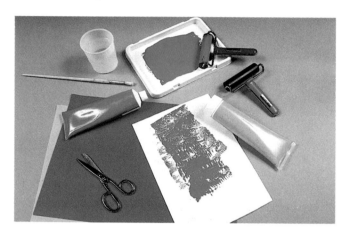

1 Squeeze some paint or ink into the tray. Coat the roller with the paint or ink and transfer it on to the printing sheet.

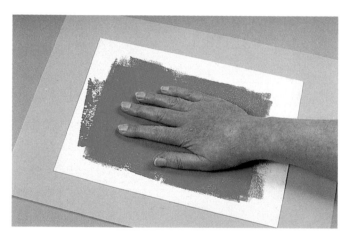

2 Spread the colour evenly with the roller and press your hand flat on to the printing sheet.

3 Now place the whole of the palm of your hand down firmly on to a sheet of paper to obtain a print.

4 Take another sheet of paper and place it over the impression of your hand in the paint or ink on the printing sheet.

5 Rub the back of your hand gently over the paper, using light pressure.

6 When you lift the paper, it will show a negative image.

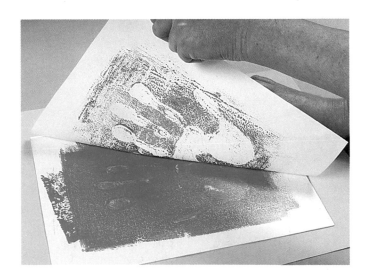

7 A positive and negative hand print.

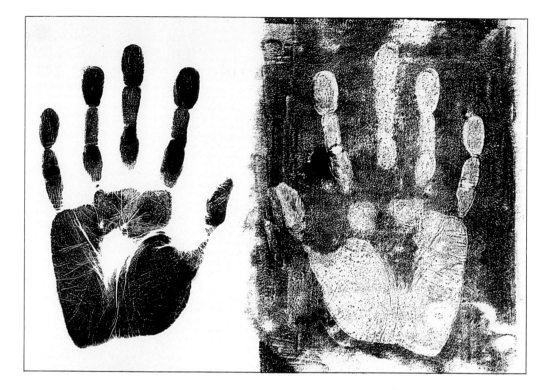

8 A pattern of hand prints, using different coloured inks on a white background.

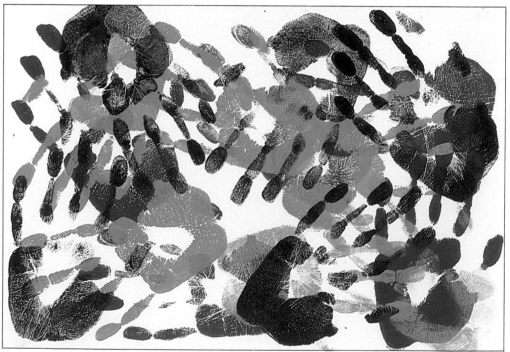

Smudge prints

A smudge print is made between the folds of a piece of paper. When the colours blend into each other, the results can be very unexpected.

You will need paper and different coloured paints.

1 Fold a piece of paper in half, then open it out.

2 Dribble some paint on to one half of the paper, in a pattern. The paint should be quite thick, yet wet enough to spread on the paper.

3 Refold the paper and smooth the folded sheet gently with the back of your hand.

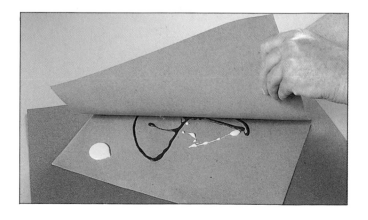

4 When you open the paper you will have, on the other half of the sheet, a symmetrical, reverse image of your pattern.

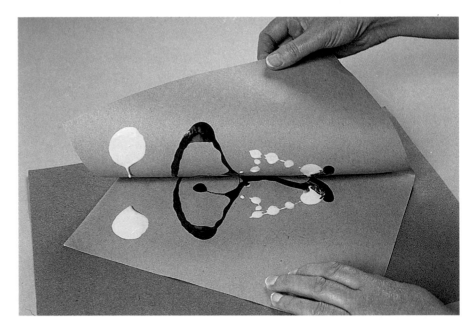

5 *Two Hobby-Horses*
The finished picture.

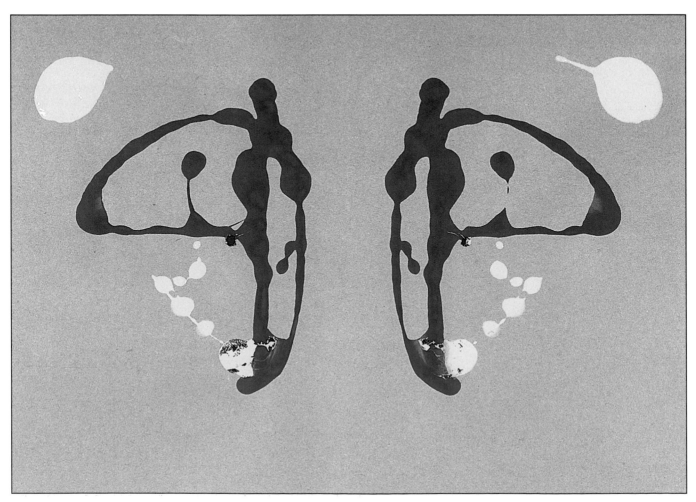

6 Your print may be the start of another picture. This multi-coloured smudge print could be turned into a mask by adding some features with a paintbrush when the print is dry.

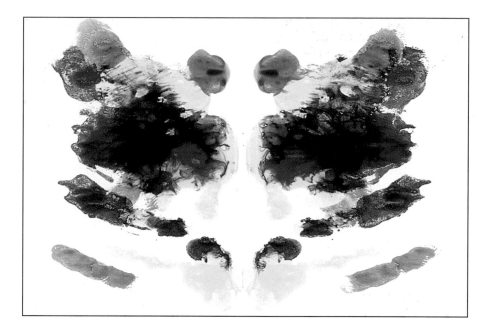

7 *A Butterfly*
Acrylic paints on a background of blue metallic paper.

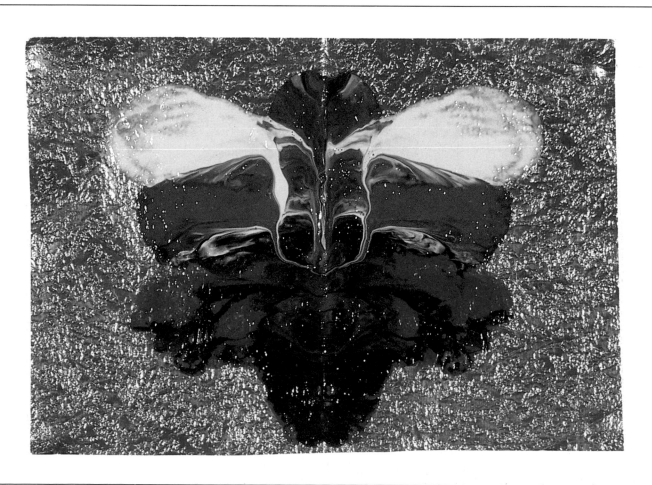

Junk prints

An assortment of bits and pieces such as matchboxes, pipe-cleaners, corks, pieces of wood, scraps of fabric and cardboard tubes can be used for printing.

Experiment by using different objects and different surfaces – for example, use the ends as well as the sides of a matchbox.

You will need printing inks or thick poster paints, paper, a sponge and an old saucer for each ink or paint colour, and your chosen 'junk materials'.

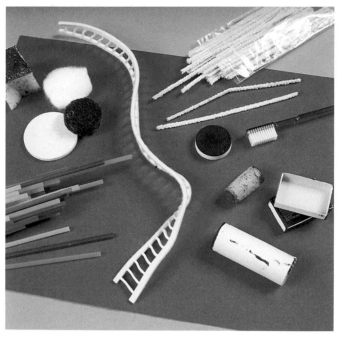

1 (Above) Ready for printing with 'junk materials'.

2 (Left) A sponge on a saucer holds the paint well and makes a good printing pad. Place the sponge in the saucer and pour paint or ink on to it. Coat your 'junk materials' with colour by pressing them into the paint – or ink-soaked sponge.

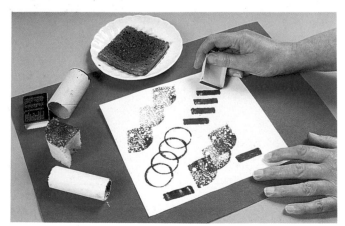

3 Printing on white paper using a matchbox, a piece of sponge and cardboard tubes. The same print can be made many times.

4 The finished design.

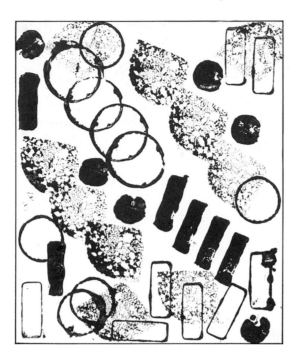

5 You can make large pictures by using only 'junk materials'. Can you see how this 'peacock' was made?

Block printing: clay blocks

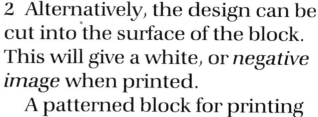

Once you have experimented with ready-made surfaces and used their natural shapes and textures, the next step is to create your own.

Printing blocks can be made in two ways:

1 A block can be built up by sticking on different textures and shapes. This will give a *positive image* of the design.

2 Alternatively, the design can be cut into the surface of the block. This will give a white, or *negative image* when printed.

A patterned block for printing can be made with modelling clay. You will need paints, a sponge and an old saucer for each paint colour, paper, modelling clay, a modelling tool, lollipop stick or teaspoon, and a wet rag.

1 Take a ball of modelling clay and thump it gently on to a flat surface, so that one side of the clay is flat. Make a pattern on the flat surface of the clay with your tool, lollipop stick or teaspoon handle.

2 Coat the patterned surface with paint. Now print a pattern. You can wipe the clay clean with the wet rag before printing it again in a different colour.

3 (Right) The finished design – overprinting lighter colours with a darker colour.

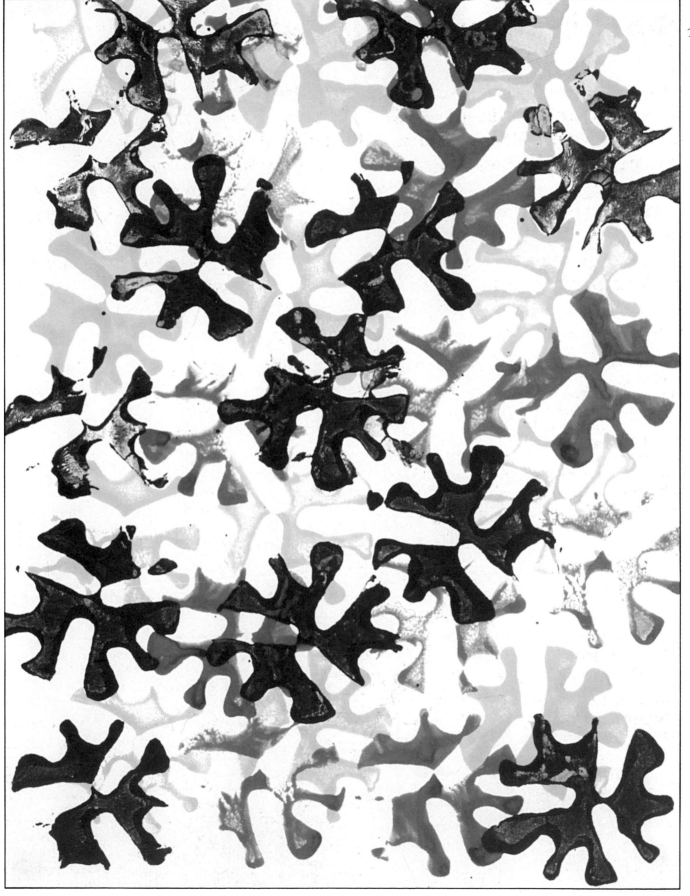

You will need card, pieces of sponge, a ballpoint pen, scissors, glue, a glue brush, paints, a sponge and an old saucer for each paint colour, and paper.

1 Draw some shapes on the pieces of sponge and cut them out.

2 Glue each shape on to a piece of card and leave them to dry.

3 (Right) Charge the sponge shapes with paint, and print a pattern on to a sheet of paper.

4 (Right) The finished design.

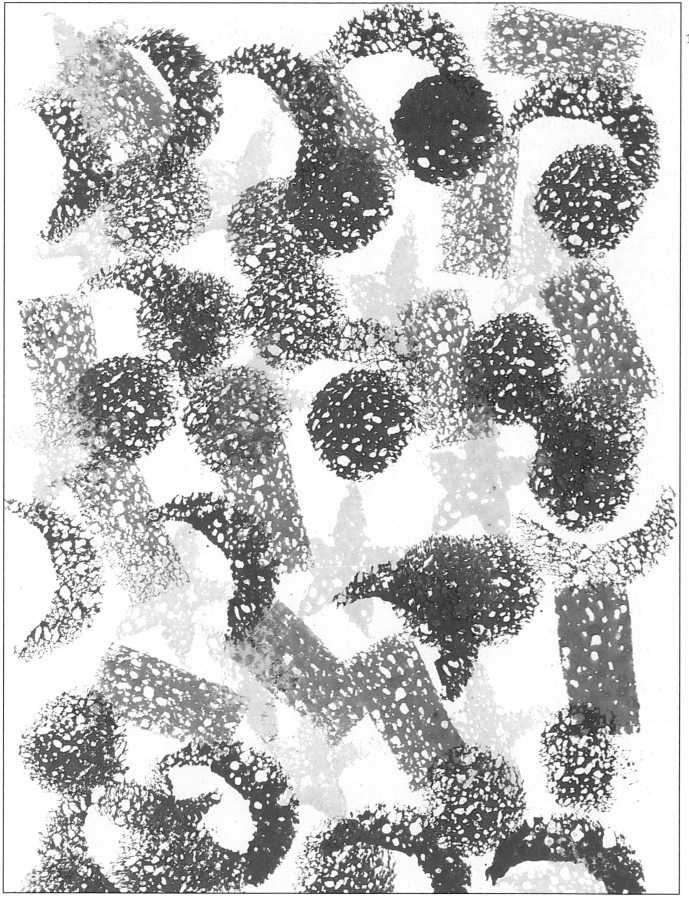

17

Block printing: felt blocks

This time a cardboard roll is used as a printing block.

You will need a cardboard tube, felt, a ballpoint pen, scissors, glue, a glue brush, paper, thick paint or printing ink, a roller, and a printing sheet.

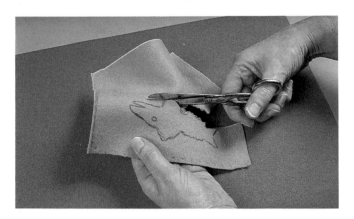

1 Draw some designs in pen on a piece of felt and carefully cut them out. Here a fish shape is being made.

2 Glue the shapes firmly on to the cardboard tube and leave to dry.

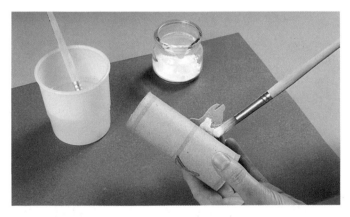

3 (Right) Using the roller, spread some paint or ink evenly on the printing sheet and roll the cardboard tube over the colour. Now roll the tube over a piece of paper to print the design. The design can be repeated as many times as necessary.

4 (Right) *An Underwater Scene* The finished design. Experiment by printing your design on wet paper – a damp paper towel (from a kitchen roll) may give an interesting result.

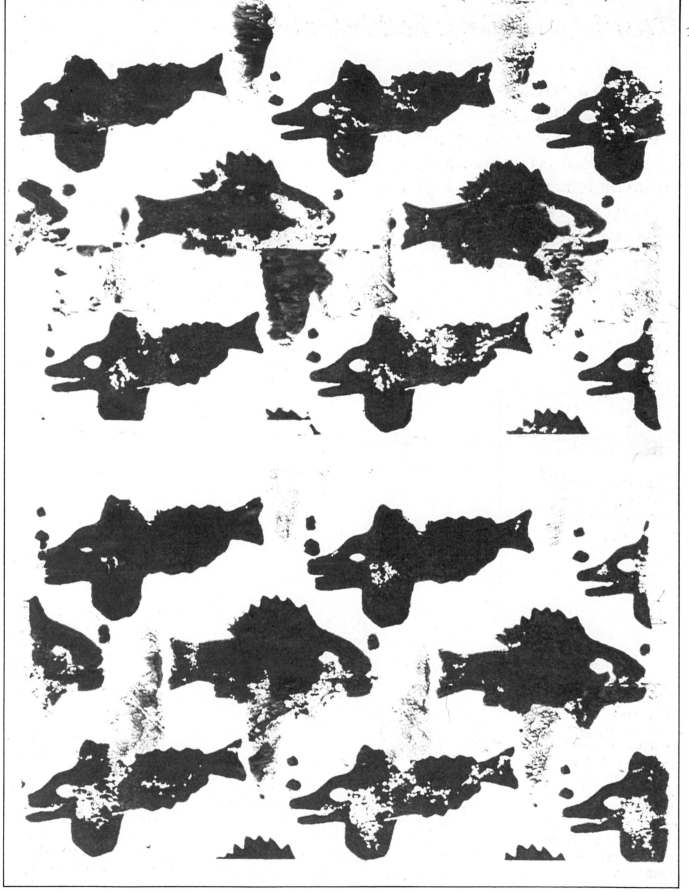

Block printing: polystyrene blocks

This idea uses a polystyrene tile (the kind used for ceilings) as a printing block.

You will need a smooth, lightweight polystyrene tile, a felt-tip pen, a pencil, printing inks, a plastic tray, two rollers, and paper.

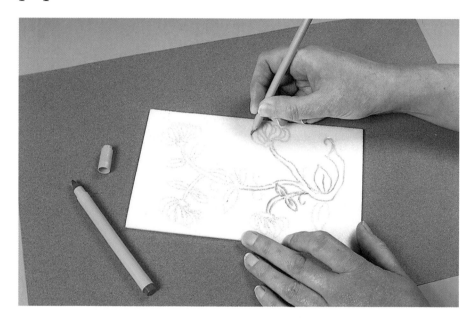

1 First, draw a design on the polystyrene tile lightly in felt-tip pen. When the design is completed, go over it again by drawing heavily with the sharp point of the pencil. This will impress the design into the surface of the tile.

2 Soak one roller evenly with ink, and ink your tile block. The design will show white.

3 Place the block face down on to a sheet of paper.

4 Gently roll over the block with the clean roller.

5 Lift the block carefully to see your print.

6 The finished design.

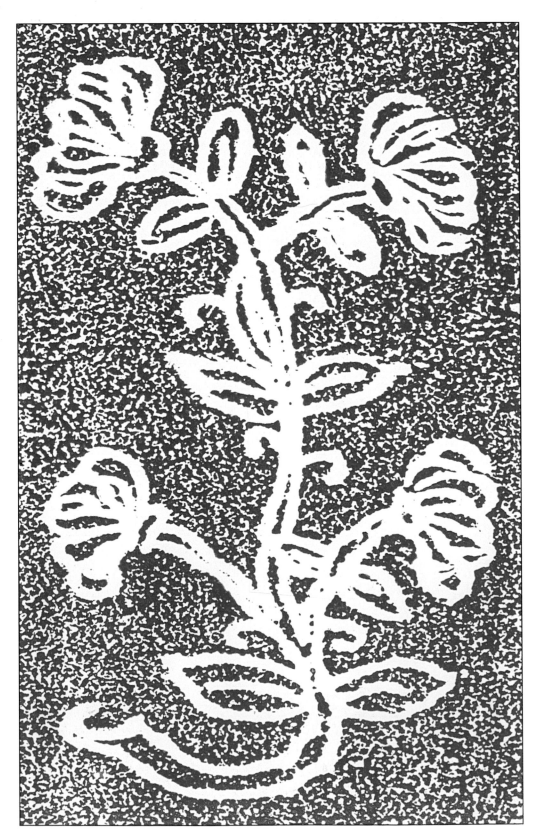

7 It may be possible to take a second print without adding more ink. This will give a lighter and often more subtle effect.

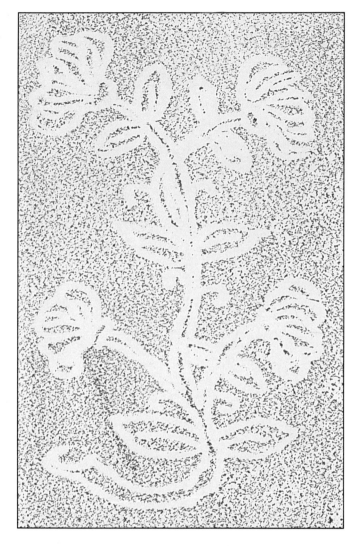

8 Printing with two colours. Try printing with a lighter colour first, then . . . . . .

9 ......overprint with a darker colour.

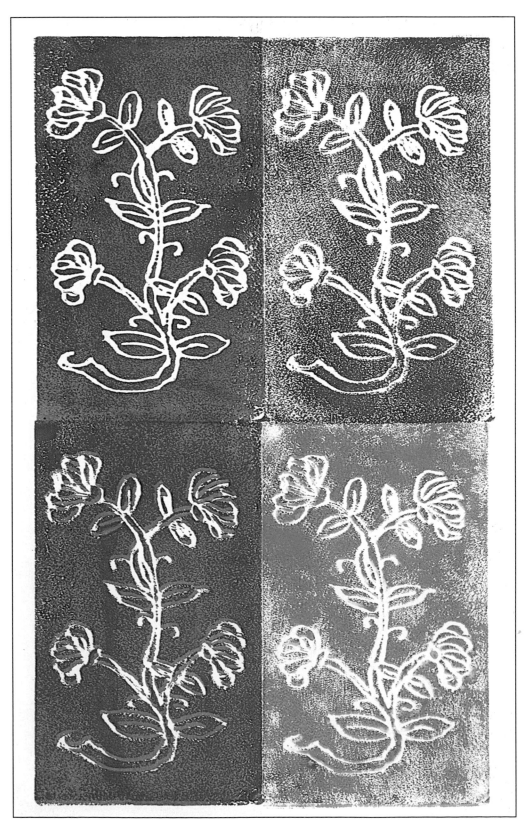

Block printing: card blocks

With thin card, it is possible to make a block which can be used many times. Topics and project work can be illustrated using this technique.

You will need a pen or pencil, scissors, thin card, glue, a glue brush, a plastic tray, printing inks, paper clips, a printing sheet, a roller, and paper.

Activity 1 Overprinting

1 Draw and cut out the shapes which make up your design and glue them on to a sheet of card. Leave to dry.

2 Place a sheet of paper over the design. Soak the roller with ink. Hold the paper steady, using the paper clips, and roll carefully over the paper. The design of the card block will slowly appear.

Activity 2
Printing with the inked block

1 This time the card block itself is inked. Remember to apply the ink evenly with the roller. Lay the block face down on to a sheet of paper. Press the block gently, to make sure a good print is transferred on to the paper.

2 (Left) Lift the block carefully to reveal your print.

3 (Right) The finished design, inspired by an embroidered cloak from Peru. c. 500 B.C.

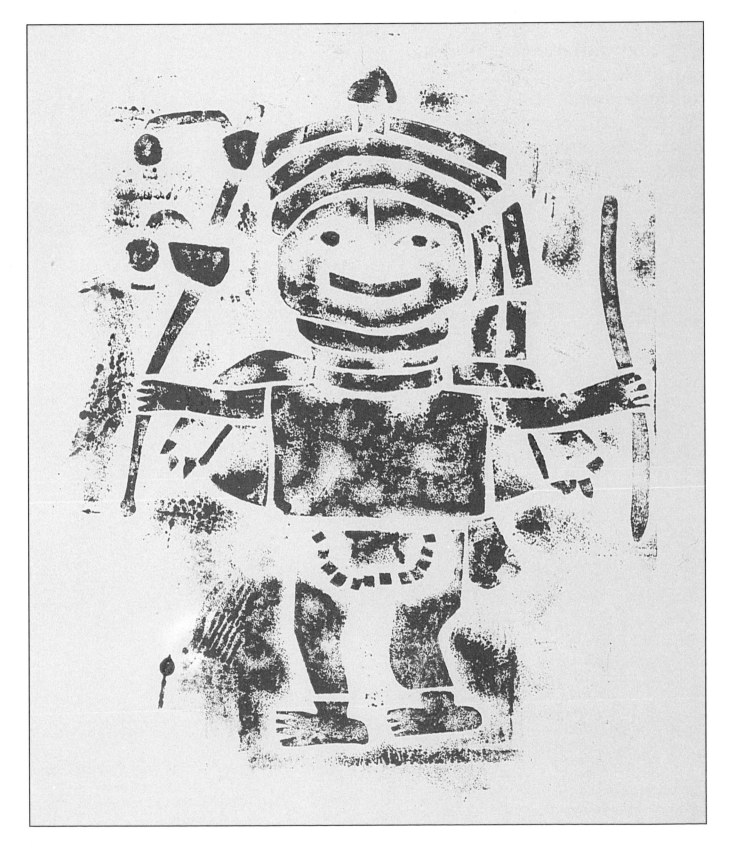

 # *Block printing: paper blocks*

Try using paper instead of card for constructing a block. Torn paper gives a better effect for natural designs such as trees and landscapes; cut paper is best for man-made objects such as houses and boats.

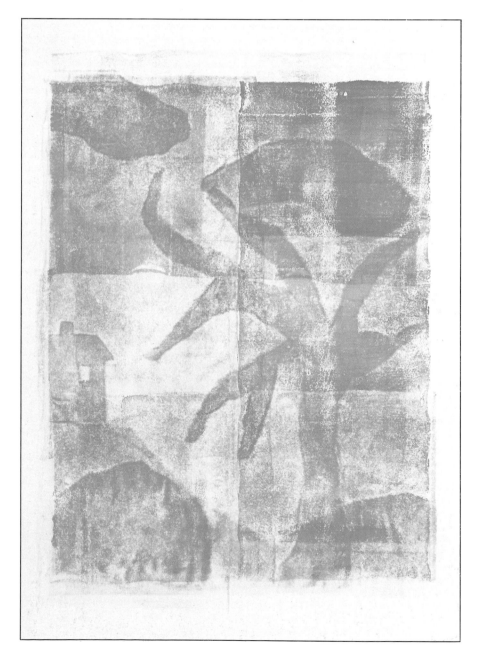

1 (Left) An overprint from a paper block.

2 (Right) The same block printed in yellow on a red background.

Block printing: corrugated card blocks

Creating a block with corrugated card gives interesting results.

You will need a pencil, scissors, corrugated card, glue, a glue brush, card, a plastic tray, printing inks, a printing sheet, a roller, and paper.

1 Draw and cut out from the corrugated card the shapes which make up your design. Glue them on to a sheet of ordinary, smooth card and leave to dry.

2 Soak the roller with ink and roll it evenly over the card block. Use more than one colour if you like.

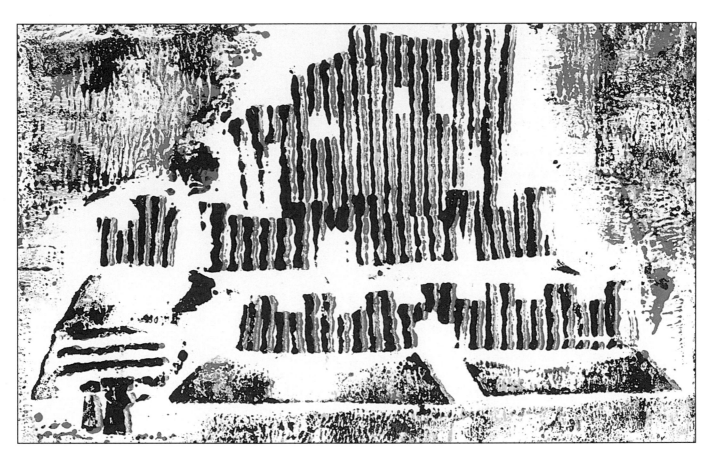

3 *Norman Keep*
The printed design,
made by laying the
inked card block on to
a sheet of paper.

Block printing: string blocks

String blocks can be used to outline a design and will give a strong, positive line image when printed.

You will need card, a pencil, glue, a glue brush, string, printing inks, two rollers, a plastic tray, a printing sheet, and paper.

1 Draw a picture in pencil on the card. Glue string around the outline of your design and leave to dry.

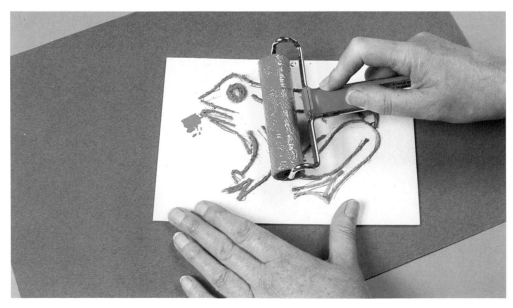

2 Soak one roller with ink. Ink the string block carefully. It may be necessary to do this twice as the string will absorb much of the ink on the first attempt.

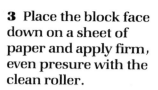

3 Place the block face down on a sheet of paper and apply firm, even presure with the clean roller.

4 Lift the block carefully to reveal the design.

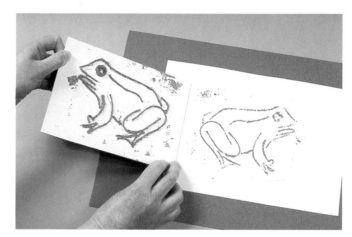

5 Experiment with different coloured inks and papers.

34

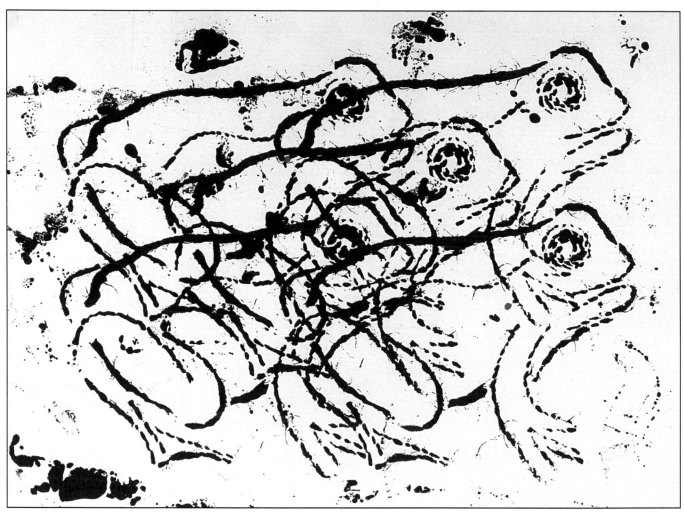

6 *The Frog Family*

This technique creates interesting textures as well as subtle variations in tone and colour.

The finished block is flexible, yet can be used for printing many times.

To make the block you will need strong paper, a pencil, a tube of PVA glue with a nozzle applicator, printing inks, a printing sheet, two rollers, and paper.

1 (Right) First draw a picture on the strong paper. Now carefully dribble the glue along the lines of your design. The glue will come out in varying thicknesses. This uneven ow will add interest to the finished print. Leave to dry.

2 *Galloping Into Battle* Spread ink on to the printing sheet and soak one roller with colour. Place your design face down on the wet surface. Roll gently and evenly over the back of the block with the clean roller. Print the inked block in the usual way. Experiment by adding different coloured inks.

A print may also be obtained from the impression of the block which has been left in the ink on the printing sheet.

3 *Galloping Home*
A negative image taken from the printing sheet.

Mono-printing, unlike blockprinting which can be repeated many times, gives only one print from the original design. Once it has been printed, you can take further prints, but the original picture has changed and no two mono-prints will be exactly the same.

You will need a printing sheet, paper, a pencil, printing ink, and a roller.

1 First draw a design on a sheet of paper. Roll some ink evenly on to the printing sheet and place the sheet of paper on to the wet surface, design side up.

2 Draw over the outlines of the picture in pencil. Work quickly, using gentle but firm pressure.

3 Peel back the paper carefully to reveal your print.

It may be possible to take a second print from . . .

4 . . . the print on the paper or . . .

5 . . . the impression on the printing sheet.

Which one gives a negative print?

6 (Right) *St Paul's Cathedral* The finished design.

This is a second example of mono-printing.

You will need a printing sheet, a plastic tray, a roller, printing inks, an old rag, an old saucer, and paper.

1 Using the roller, spread some ink evenly over the printing sheet.

2 Use the rag to make a design by wiping away the ink.

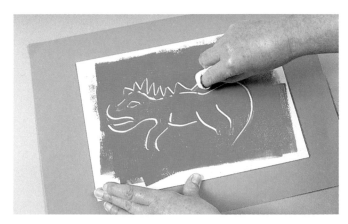

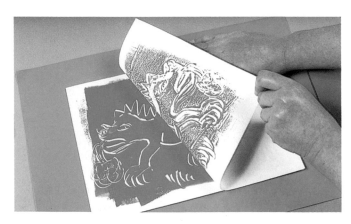

3 Take a print. Remember to smooth gently over the paper with the back of the hand.

4 (Above) This method of printing will give a negative print.

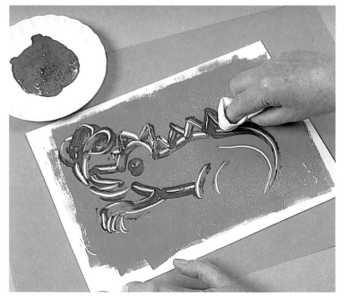

5 (Left) Experiment by applying some colour to the rag before drawing the design.

6 and 7 (Above and
right) If the ink is
sufficiently wet, you
may be able to take a
print from a print!

Having used this book you will have discovered how different printing materials behave, and you will have worked with many different types of papers and textured surfaces.

Here are a few more activities for you to try.

1 Try to make a picture which combines two or more of the ideas contained in this picture. For example, you could make a rag print design and decorate it with a variety of junk material prints.

2 Using thick paints and a brush, make a mask by painting only half the face. If the paper is folded, you can make a smudge print to give you a complete mask (see photograph **1**)!

1 A smudge print mask on a green background

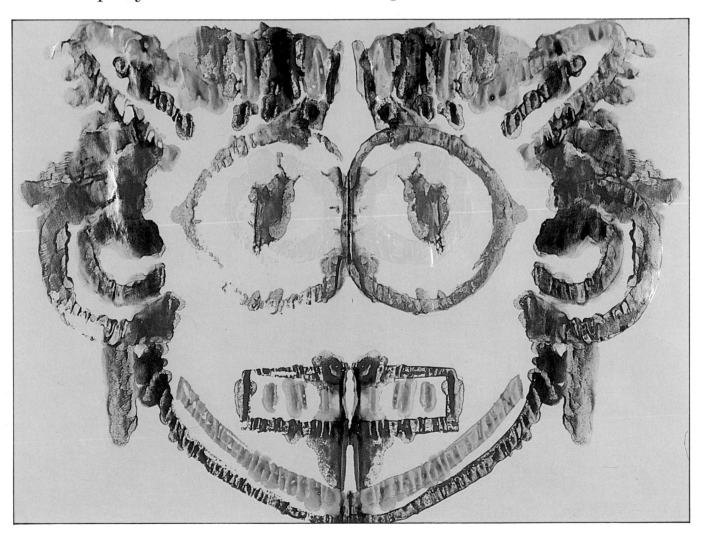

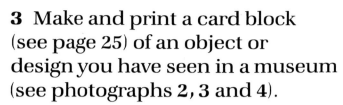

3 Make and print a card block
(see page 25) of an object or
design you have seen in a museum
(see photographs **2**, **3** and **4**).

2 An overprint of a
lion design created
from a museum
sketch.

3 The printed lion's head.

4 A repeated pattern, alternating the two methods.

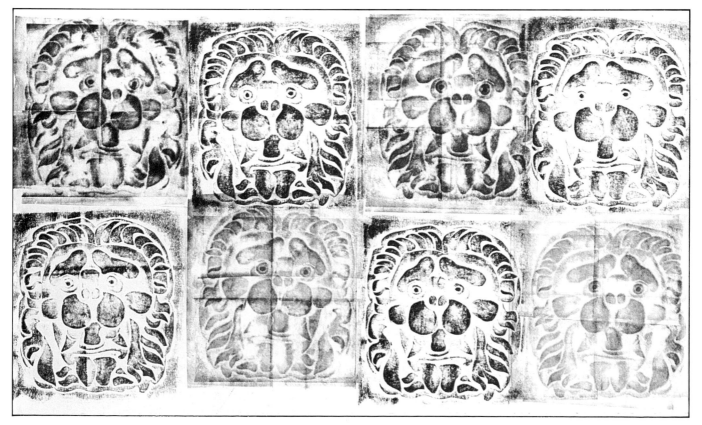

4 String pulls

For this final idea you will need a piece of string about 1m long, a paintbrush, paper, coloured drawing inks, and an old saucer (see photographs **5**, **6** and **7**).

5 Ink the piece of string, leaving some of it clean so that there is a small length to hold.

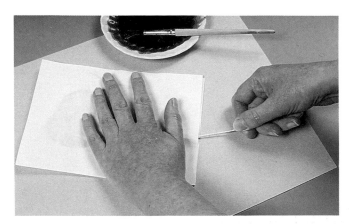

6 Place the string inside a folded sheet of paper, curling it inside the fold. Close the folded paper and hold it firmly with one hand. Now gently pull the string out.

7 Attractive swirly patterns can be produced. Try again using the same string, but do not add any more ink.

Adhesives

PVA adhesives (e.g. Alocryl and Marvin) can be thinned with water or mixed with powder paints to produce an acrylic paint. Two adhesives supplied in containers with nozzles are Arnold Cream Adhesive and UHU Clear Glue.

Paper and card

Most stationers stock a range of papers and card suitable for use with the activities in this book.

Printing inks

Some recommended water-based inks are: Arnold Multiprint; Berol Print Inks; Reeves Block Printing Watercolours.

Printing rollers

These are obtainable in a variety of widths – 10cm width is an average size, and recommended for the activities in this book.

All the materials listed above can be obtained from an artists' materials stockist, or ordered through a schools' supplier such as E J Arnold & Sons Ltd, Parkside Lane, Dewsbury Road, Leeds LS11 5TD.